Writers praise *Buried Pennies*:

In this extraordinary book of poems, Pete Olevnik speaks in a voice both nuanced and wise. The poems delve deeply into childhood visits with Polish grandparents in Chicago, and growing up in Indiana surrounded by a family of hard-working, plain-spoken people. Love is ever present. The unforgettable "Letter to Irene," for example, commemorates a life spent helping others.

These 35 poems—some superbly illustrated by the author—range far, from Bosnia in the Balkans to Asheville in the Appalachian Mountains. All in all, a virtuoso performance that will stay with you long after you have closed the book.

– Mike Ross
Author *Small Engine Repair*
Instructor, Osher Lifelong Learning Institute, UNC Asheville


Peter Olevnik writes with an artist's eye for detail and a deep reverence for all life. Whether writing about the death of a parent or sister or about a decaying carcass, he explores our often complex connections with all living things. "I will mourn your loss as mine," he writers in the poem "Carrion."

His poems find the holy places in the everyday: the stranger at Ingles grocery, a dying tree, and a city destroyed by war. To read Peter's poems is to discover our place in the world, a world that the poet writes about with precision, insight, and love. These poems come from a poet who has lived life fully and looked closely at the world he inhabits and at his fellow travelers. They will give you a sense of belonging and reveal a world you may have overlooked.

– Pat Riviere-Seel
Author, *The Serial Killer's Daughter*

ArsPoetica is an imprint of Pisgah Press, established in 2011 to publish and promote works of quality offering original ideas and insight into the human condition and the world around us.

Copyright © 2017 Pete Olevnik
Printed in the United States of America

Cover painting by Pete Olevnik
Book design & layout by A. D. Reed, Pisgah Press

All artwork reproduced in this book
is by Pete Olevnik

All rights reserved. No part of this publication may be reproduced, stored in a retrieval system, or transmitted, in any form or by any means, electronic, mechanical, photocopying, recording, or otherwise, without the prior written permission of Pisgah Press, except in the case of quotations in critical articles or reviews.

Library of Congress Cataloging-in-Publication Data
Olevnik, Peter
---------------

Library of Congress Control Number: 2017938905

ISBN 13: 978-1942016335
ISBN 10: 1942016336
Poetry/General

First Edition
April 2017

# Buried Pennies

Poems

Pete Olevnik

# Dedication

For Judy, to whom I owe so much.

# Contents

## Book I. Ties

A Train Ride ..................................................................... 5
The Coffee Pot .................................................................. 7
The Cruller ....................................................................... 8
Pennies ........................................................................... 10
The Concertina ............................................................... 11
Death Be Near ................................................................ 13
Engagement .................................................................... 14
Like a Switch .................................................................. 16
A Letter to Irene ............................................................. 18
When He Left, He Left the Door Ajar ........................... 20
Father ............................................................................. 21
Chicken Soup ................................................................. 22
The Call .......................................................................... 24
The Smoke-Filled Side ................................................... 25
A Gift ............................................................................. 28

## Book II. Place

A Hole in the Sky .......................................................... 33
Ingles Grocery ................................................................ 34
Birdman of Ashevile ...................................................... 37
A Collie Named Gypsy .................................................. 39
The Creek ....................................................................... 40
City of Brotherly Love ................................................... 41
A Rabbit ......................................................................... 42
The Bridge at Mostar ..................................................... 45
At the Coffee Shop ........................................................ 47
Hoosier Defined ............................................................. 48

## Book III. Musing

| | |
|---|---:|
| A Poem | 53 |
| Like a Raindrop | 54 |
| Remembering Ann | 55 |
| A Meditation | 57 |
| Faith | 58 |
| A Holy Place | 61 |
| The Carrion | 62 |
| Sunset | 63 |

## Book IV. Addendum

| | |
|---|---:|
| A Fable Revisited | 67 |
| Rumpelstiltskin Revisited | 68 |

| | |
|---|---:|
| About the Author | 71 |

# Buried Pennies

Poems

# BOOK I

# TIES

Peter Olevnik

## A Train Ride

Saturday before sunrise
we climbed the steel steps
of Number 8, going to Chicago.
Across the tracks were rows of black
buildings, with cornices perched
like birds of prey, profiled by
rows of stalking street lights.

We were on our way.
Absorbed in the coach's slumbering nest
and the rhythmic tap of wheels,
as they kissed the tracks,
we soon fell asleep.

We rose with the first sliver
of morning light, stretching
to wipe away the night,
heard the wheels of our coach car
creating a thundering staccato
rumbling across the Illinois Central
crossing just before Torrance Avenue.

Soon we would be in South Chicago,
streaming along tracks that took us past
gray expanses of aging steel mills;
tired, compacted two-flat homes;
lines of dirty, rusted cars and
sky raining a constant pall of ash.

Stony Island, the conductor announced.
Not a depot, but a rail yard.
Mom took us in tow across the tracks
to a waiting, wicker-seated streetcar,
soon on its way bouncing and swaying
as it passed long blocks of shops, with iron gates,
that stretched across their prows.

Descending the streetcar steps,
into the warmth of morning sun,
we rushed past rows of tidy Polish homes,
with tiny yards and narrow passage ways.
We had arrived. Grandmother
pulled us into her warm, embracing self,
letting us know we belonged.

## The Coffee Pot

Immense, it stood, galvanized blue
and speckled white,
on top of an iron kitchen stove,
in grandma's Chicago two-flat, bottom floor.
For us kids she allowed a cup.
Only lots'a milk, she would say,
in her Polish-broken-English.

What drew us mostly, set center,
atop a large, round, kitchen table was
a heaping platter of pastries,
filled with paczki, jelly-filled,
twists of cinnamon sweet rolls
and deep-fried chocolate donuts.

I'll let it go for twenty-five-fifty, he said
at a highway antique store.
What caught my eye on a shelf
was the galvanized blue coffee pot, a bit pitted,
like the one I long ago recalled. Too much,
I said, Just seeing it was enough for me.

## The Cruller

A confection at grandmother's
on Sunday after church—
always served fresh.

She starts with rich risen
pastry dough, color of cream,
and kneading—like clay
for a potter's wheel—
rolling it over a bed of flour
on her kitchen counter,

cutting the ecru-silky dough
into ribbons, like columns,
then into rows, making squares
through which she makes centered slices.

Of the children, she chooses me,
like passing on a bit of herstory,
to twist the pastries
one-by-one through their slits
into bows, just like threading needles,
she enlightens me.

She delicately lifts each pastry,
floating it into a cauldron of boiling oil,
transforming it into a delicate
flaky curl she dusts with a cloud
of confectionery sugar.

She fills the platter full
wth pastries, like butterfly bows,
as children sit, in glee, with powdered faces.
For me a memory of where I belong.

## Pennies

Jerry and I buried them
under the front porch.

The house still there.
Jerry's gone,
mom and dad,
aunts and uncles too.

There's much I'd like to know,
but no one left to ask.

Perhaps, some day,
I'll go back
dig up those pennies.

## The Concertina

In a fading photograph,
a scene in a neighbor's
South Chicago backyard,
he is sitting by an open door,
like a statue caught by time,
concertina on his lap.
It was the 1920s.
I sat—long time wondering
what song he played, and
who might have been his
invisible guests.

Suddenly, I was there,
heard him play, his music
wafting through the air,
with the smell of sausages frying,
rounds of wine and beer,
mixed with cheer and laughter.

As I gazed into the photograph,
instantly, it was a Sunday afternoon
in our Fort Wayne, Indiana, home.
Mother was making dinner;
father sitting on a couch,
playing the concertina, his fingers
fluttering over the keys,
inviting our listening to streams
of mazurkas and polkas.

As I turned, I see the case
placed high on the cellar shelf,
its silver corners tarnished,
the concertina lying in its crumbling case.

It was then I knew
we had lived too far apart.

## Death Be Near

The floating dock seemed an apt destination,
not beyond the ability I long ago remembered.
I began to swim, buoyed by family
gathering by the shore.

As I approached the dock,
each stroke seemed to make it further still.
Arms like anvils pulling me down,
in terror, I began to drown
wouldn't reach the ladder.
What a struggle to hoist my body up,
call an ambulance too late,
come together to my funeral?
thoughts like these
racing through my mind.

Desperate, I lunged for the ladder rung,
Clung.
Pulling myself up like a saturated mop,
collapsing on the floor of the dock.
Rising, when able, waving in cheer,
(not wanting to blacken their day)
I know I must plunge again to shore.

## Engagement

It was a solemn scene
in an aging photograph,
of a house in Indiana,
its porch, a family and their guest.

The house, a tattered overcoat
hung with little care, little warmth,
recycled, like an evening shift.
(If you look, you'll see a rainspout missing.)

The father peering out to me,
standing behind a post, as if trapped,
a weathered man, a gray mustache
between an owl-like nose and a tuneless smile.

The daughter, like a dancer,
quick to smile like a sunray passing through a cloud,
one hand on an opened door,
the other, a fist in sisterly mock reproach
of tangled affection.

The son, like a knight, at his mother's side,
his red wagon a rostrum,
cradling a toy shotgun,
aiming it at a foe he has yet to know.

The guest, my corsage at her breast,
decorously dressed in a navy-blue suit,
her fingers at the railing like piano keys
wistfully staring as if peering
through the mist of her being.

In the camera's shadow
I took a picture of their eyes,
agent of their minds.

## Like A Switch

Much later in my life,
it was sudden, I recalled,
from within a forgotten
room inside my mind,
like a circuitous train ride
from juncture to juncture
on its way to recollection.

To my wife, innocently said
Hurry Hon, or we'll be late,
I urged, in a tone unappraised.
Suddenly, she began to cry.
Perplexed, I asked,
anything I said?
It was then the memory recalled.

My mother nervously rushing,
we kids sitting in our father's
black Buick touring car, in order by seniority
determining where each should sit,
father, in intolerant exasperation,
began to blow the auto's horn.
Inexplicably, I felt her sense of servitude,

In a dream, I'm climbing
a floating helix tower.
Ascending its twisting stairs,
I search its countless courses.
two are labeled attributes:
compassion is the first,
intolerance next.

Like a switch I turn it off.

## A Letter to Irene

Your hurts no longer:
too many for your soul to bear.
Nobody there to tell you what was to be—
not the girl-child running to tragedy.
You would never find release.

In child rivalry, I couldn't see
already your inevitability—
a tree that would never take root.

With children of your own, returning home,
distance seemed too great a chasm—
one too late for reaching you;
an embrace would turn to ice.

A mother who gave you life,
you kindly cared for her doleful soul,
until she escaped in death,
a path you too early followed.

You choose to die alone.
Yet, in your death was your strength.
Only once when we gathered to honor you,
you opened your heart: told us:
I no longer have a future.
Shortly after that you died.

I spread your ashes where you hoped to go:
a warm and gentle, sunlit, ocean beach:
a trip in life you never took.

With love
Your brother

## When He Left, He Left the Door Ajar

He came home, lay down
across the covers—then died.
What was one to make of it?

It's been a while
since we never talked,
no fishing trips
to fill the pages, but still...

He was proud
when I could name
a locomotive's parts.
At the railroad engine house,
I would always be Pete's kid.

Once he took the lot of us
on a trip to Niagara Falls,
faulting us for buying souvenirs,
not listening to
the power of the falls.

He never told my sisters and me
much about himself;
I do not know, my son
might feel the same toward me.

# Father

Hurry home, the caller urged.
In seconds I was in my car,
fears spinning in my head.
He had a bad heart,
but had passed these calls before.

My headlights caught site
of a neighborhood church,
a place long forgotten.
Obeying a sudden urge,
I parked, then entered.

Rows of flickering candles,
a few shadowed figures in the pews,
I found a place to sit,
confronting a forgotten time.
A stranger in a stranger's house.

I asked this not be my father's time,
then quickly left.
At the curb a car out of place,
with open door and lights left on.
It must be the doctor, I thought.

Up the steps I ran to the bedroom
where he lay, his mouth agape.
A troubling thought crept in:
He wasn't dressed for death,
prayer didn't stop the clock.

## Chicken Soup

It was a special time at the family home
in South Chicago's Polish neighborhood.
Grandmother, my mother and her sisters,
absorbed at the downstairs kitchen
coal stove crowded with pots of cooking soup,
sizzling pans of sausages and nearby
trays of rising dough; aromas
wafting through the kitchen's tangled air.

With a bowl of chicken soup mother handed me,
and her all-purpose admonition, *You can go now,
but remember to be good.*
Soup in hand, I took the steps upstairs
to a hushed crowd of visitors, some aside
in prayer, murmuring, others stilled
in rows of folding chairs.

At one end of the parlor, under a row
of lace-curtained windows a casket rested,
church kneeler placed at its side
for me to see grandfather sound asleep,
dressed in a suit he rarely wore,
large hands jutting beyond the sleeves,
mustache-crowded face.

Forgetting my chicken soup,
I spilled it down his pillow case.
Mother took me aside. *Grandfather died.*
*He won't be back*, with tenderness, she said.
*Funeral is tomorrow at the church across the street.*
Her words unleashed a torrent flooding through my mind.
like a door suddenly thrust open:
I knew some day I would die.

As quickly opened, the door slammed shut.

## The Call

It came late

    COME HOME!

At the hospital—a double room—
    near the door

Her skin the color of straw
Breathing in fitful gasps.
    Slowing, slowing down

I cursed the nurse's perfunctory checks
Couldn't she see how pointless!
But it was I
I came late.

    THEN

    Her one last grasp for air
    Nailed to my memory

        In the room—at the other bed
        Radio ON: incessant—mindless—chattering
        (the curtain suddenly SWOOSHED close)

Mother would never mind.

## The Smoke-Filled Side

I entered the gingerbread-gabled depot
through a dark oak side door,
clutching my ticket
as if it might fly away.
My mother told me, this time,
I must take the train, alone,
to grandmother's funeral.

Handing it to the agent who,
sitting at an ancient desk behind
a brass-grilled window, stamped it
saying she'd be running late today,
catching up on the way.
I found a seat amidst two rows
of church-stiff benches. In the midday
depot silence, I waited.

Like a flock of grazing sheep,
stirred before a quake, the depot
must have felt the shake as the train
had just passed Clinton Street.
The depot master knew, sending us
to the platform there to see approaching
the massive iron, one-eyed face of
a steaming locomotive coming to rest.

Climbing the passenger car steps,
I heard the conductor say
Chicago to your left. I quickly found a seat,
would soon discover my view hampered,
as I had picked the engine's smoke-filled side.

Just past Plymouth, suddenly,
the speeding train came to an unexpected stop.
Sitting the longest while, explanation not forthcoming,
I got off, walking to the front and saw
wrapped around the steaming engine face,
like an insect on a windshield splayed,
a car, two riders, surely dead.
I saw their startled, disbelieving faces,
then was told to get back on the train.
Stunned, I sat, my mind struggling
to find a place within its darkest chambers
for the tragedy to reside and routes
within to comprehend.

Hours later the tragic train
begun again its final destination
and I, forlorn, arrived at the station.
With relief I saw my mother who earlier left
to be at her dying mother's side.
In the funeral home amidst muted conversations
and sentinelly placed bouquets, grandmother lay,
dressed in a pearl-colored gown unlike
the faded housedress she had often worn.

When we children, in secret, gathered
in grandmother's basement walk-in closet,
long before, sharing our deepest secrets,
talk of death had meant the screams we heard
on Sunday night radio mystery shows,
where people died whom we would never know.
How short is our span of time to understand.

## A Gift

I asked my granddaughter
if she would like to ride with me
to the mall for a gift I want to buy
for a friend who had done a favor
for me. When asked why, I said,
*It's the proper thing to do.*

Taking this as a teaching moment,
I told her *Everything has its cost;
nothing is free.*

Suddenly, I was back
with my father, in his bitterness,
a casualty of the Great Depression
admonishing me my child's request,
with those very words
I had unwittingly uttered.

to which, my granddaughter replied,
*But my mother's love is free.*

Peter Olevnik

# BOOK II
# Place

# Peter Olevnik

## A Hole in the Sky

An aging oak tree limb
loomed above my house.
I called a cutter who climbed it
informing me your tree is dying
and should come down.

As he scaled up, his steel cleats
pierced the tree-bark flesh
of what I perceived was a blood-like ooze
flowing from its wounds.

Before long a snow-like flow appeared
in the bark, like tears flowing from its pores.
The invader, a powder beetle dining
on the oak tree's flesh.

It became a crime scene: giant logs,
like appendages, scattered by the cutter
at the bottom of the hill.

He cut the tree in sections,
climbing it like a cathedral, taking it down
stone by stone, as at the Parthenon,
where its body, like tinker toys,
was ready for reassembling.
But the tree is down.

What remains: a stump that's become a shrine,
weathered in ivy, in symbiotic union
with a shroud of limestone colored lichen.

There is now a hole in the sky.

## Ingles Grocery

At the store's coffee counter
there was a stranger ahead of me.
Seemed pleasant enough.

In no hurry, if asked, I'd claim
a modicum of generosity.
Yet, this stranger in front of me
drew from me no animosity,
but a feeling I didn't understand:
intolerance, or some vestigial apprehension?

In the time the server took
to complete his request,
I recognized her, having often stopped
for coffee there.

I sometimes saw her at a table
with an older man
I took to be her grandfather
in uniform—as the store security guard.
He never smiled, never acknowledged
I was even there.

## Buried Pennies

As a boy, from the other side of the tracks,
friends and I were arrested once by the police
on a robbery charge, were separately held,
interrogated for several hours,
then set free.

At my table, the stranger, on leaving,
stopped by holding out two quarters,
saying he saw them fall and knew
they were surely mine.

## Birdman of Asheville

Like a ninth-floor eagle
he peers down the streets and years
from a book-filled, three-room flat
disdainful of wealth's encumbrances,
a paperhanger's wisdom garnered
papering others' castle walls.

Perhaps, you've seen him
on his downtown-mountain-morning walk.
Asheville, the only place he's known.
With a country dancer's gait slowed
by age and minor stroke,
he's ordinary to distraction.

  As World War II chaplain
he saw war's meaningless resolution.
Master of his universe, with soul of a humanist,
he seeks peace in his tiny shop
building whimsical birdhouses in pastel hues
for posterity and for you.

During our walks, he talks of years
learning life on the porch across the street,
Thomas Wolfe's mother's boarding house,
The Old Kentucky Home,
listening to drummers tales,
prodding him on where
they might have
some little fun,

or listening to shop girls and secretaries,
staffing downtown offices and sales rooms,
sharing stories and dreams,
fleeing country hollows
to find the lure
of city living.

Like an arrow to its center, he continues, was
Patton Avenue to Pack Square where on Saturday nights
city folk and farmers filled the plaza,
their wagons and Model T's
resting hand in hand.

Then he concluded our visit.
*It's now three, time to go*, he states.
*It's time for tea with a friend
down the hall.*

# A Collie Named Gypsy

Aged roamer of his universe
to the middle of the block, arising
from the corner of my neighbor's garage,
solemnly greets the day,
plods his way across the street.

Like two seniors on a park bench,
renewing yardly fellowship,
sees me start my morning walk,
ponders, lamely walks my way.
A simple pat: my way to say hello.

Another day he stops, seems to listen.
Gently, I stroke his shaggy coat
singed with gray and patchy clouds of white,
sweep away his shedding hair.
Then he's on his way up the street.

Frail, of a different mind, he doesn't
come to me today, but hobbles to a pool
at a street-side ditch, dips his paw,
takes a drink. Does he know today's the day
my neighbor has him put to sleep?

## The Creek

At my morning window
catching my eye
was the rain sent creek,
just beyond my dooryard.

Nibbling, nudging, then etching
the loam rich soil
clinging to its edges,
it coursed its recumbent way.

So unlike the grassy crowd
climbing up its craggy sides,
the swollen creek now mirrored
the shimmering sky.

Where the street and creek met,
not taking a rectangular route,
preferring nature's less angled course,
the creek was tunneled on its way.

Beyond, they flowed
side by side,
till compelled again to divide,
their courses parting.

One unbending in direction,
the other wending
into a woods of tulip trees,
to a forest celebration.

## City of Brotherly Love

From my November window
the marble font below—now still
a sharp quiet born of intimacy
they nightly share.

Carrying plastic sacks
asleep on granite fountain beds,
homeless peer from pasteboard walls.

Where women sidewalk stand—despair
shout Jesus' name in vain
while others sit in paper vests
suck the waning sun
against the shock of coming night.

On Market Street, bleating street
where electric shops spew their sounds
into walking ears
and darkened souls in hesitation
hold paper cups for coins,
where tables set with plastic-penny fare
and hawkers tend their sidewalk cells.

A town engulfed in sprawling streets
where hallowed halls faintly echo
pleas once raised to shouts—for equality
by light of the Enlightenment.

For some, the silent fountain stones—for bed.
In silence, their souls ignored, repose.

## A Rabbit

It's just after sunrise
as I take my morning walk
stuck on a poem,
when neighborhood rabbits
are up to eat.

One is at my neighbor's
munching on a blade of grass
ears flickering nuances
on the morning air.

He is sitting sidelong
dressed in a dappled coat of umber,
black eye regarding me,
the other no doubt scanning
where he might flee.

So close, I thought I might touch him,
but became wary of his intent.
Is he greeting me? I wonder?
Will he attack me? the rabbit ponders?

Seeing I plan no harm, he jumps ahead,
anticipating my direction,
wanting me to follow.

Up the street he veers
into another neighbor's yard
resuming breakfast with a friend,
while I, alone, awaiting toast and eggs.

The two of them dismiss
any thought of me as they dine,
while I, I continued on
questioning my chosen path.

## The Bridge at Mostar

*Preface*
*The war in Bosnia Herzegovina was an international conflict that occurred between April 1992 and December 1995. Among the more than 97,000 reported killed or missing were those of the city of Mostar, many citizens of which were adherents of Islam. (Wikipedia)*


In Mostar, Ottoman Islam's western toe,
an ancient land dappled in steeples and minarets,
market stalls, metal smiths and wafts of burning incense.
From church bells' tolls and daily calls to prayer,
east met west in tapestry of sight and sound.

At the River Neretva Suleiman ordered
his architect, Hayruddin build a bridge
under pain of death should you fail.
In anticipation of its collapse,
Hayruddin prepared his own grave.
His bridge lasted more than four hundred years.

From eastern to western shore it spanned,
a single semicircle arch, like a hunter's bow,
becoming one mirrored in the stream below.
With classic symmetry, two guardian towers
at its sides, a metaphor
for ethnic and religious mutuality.

On its completion,
Mostar's youth found challenge in its height,
diving from its sides, launching a tradition,
coaxing crowds for their coins,
before plunging into the river.

Mostar caught in the vacuum vat of war
at Yugoslavia's demise,
saw neighbor states, their coterie enticed,
light the flame first wrought in nationhood
fed the fire of ethnic elimination.

Where Christian-Muslim neighbors
lived centuries side by side, the bridge
became a route of Muslim expurgation.

Driven by bombs and sniper fire,
red stained streets and night-dug graves,
Mostar's Muslims fled eastward across the bridge.
Once the sign of toleration, by calculation
the bridge was then destroyed.

In horror a message on an alley wall
was written: "I swear to God, I hope we die together."
In the shambles of ethnic purging, white stones glistened,
resting at the river's bottom.

## At The Coffee Shop

In muffled cliques and coffee cups
cozy little tattered homes,
unsuited sofas and easy chairs,
and window sills of poster piles,
a plastic rack says "Take One Free."

All this inviting you and me.
A stage for us to ply
For what I fail to comprehend
is the praying mantis' fate I see.

## Hoosier Defined

Today, I decided to find out
what "Hoosier" means.
Being from Nebraska, I decided it's
time I know.  I got into my car
heading for Churubusco, Indiana.
Since I'm not that far away, I decided
to stop the first time I saw someone
I might find to ask.

Hey, you there, what's a "Hoosier"?
He took a deep breath, like a Scottish
player at his bagpipe.
What kind'a answer you want?
Just the regular kind, I responded.
Reminded me of my uncle Clyde—
never did like him much, he answered.

I got back in my car. The damn thing wouldn't start.
I waved down a passing car.
Could you tell me what's a "Hoosier"?
He said he didn't know.
Not from these parts.  Ask a priest—they don't lie,
'less it's a Unitarian—they'd tell you one way or another,
don't much matter.  What's the question again?

Peter Olevnik

Book III

# Musing

Peter Olevnik

> *"...O that I may make improvements*
> *of this little time, before I*
> *go hence and no more ...!*
>
> James Morgan at his gallows day, 1686
> (*The Americans: The Colonial Experience*
> Daniel J. Boorstin)

## A Poem

In soil enriched by snows
and Indian bones
and leaves in fall—falling,
becoming death's microphone.

At dusk on a chilling after-rain
I pass a graveyard gate.
In stillness, but for swirling leaves,
so faintly—faintly I hear the sighs,
through the sycamores' and the oaks'
empty finger tips,
of those where I walk
among the aging alabaster rows.

That I left a poem someone may recall.

## Like A Raindrop

Old age, like a summer rain,
catches me on my morning walk,
wetting the skin of my ire
 at its coming, like a creek
spilling over the bank
of my craggy face.

I watch a silver bead,
like a pearl pendant,
drop to a sun drenched leaf
of an aging dogwood tree,
slide to a silky ledge,

      then fall

startling a more weathered kin
less kindly touched by the sun,
expelling its unexpected guest
to slip off its rutted face,

      then fall

into a shadowed underworld
landing on a haggard host
beyond sun's disregarding,

      then fall,

absorbed into a dormant soil,
waiting patiently for me.

## Remembering Ann

We drove to the memorial garden
trading memories of her,
like matching stockings
tumbling in a mindful dryer.

The only ones there besides the two of us,
the minister she never knew,
the husband and her husband's son.

In the garden a circle of sweet violets baring,
in a patch pulled back like flesh,
a shallow hole, a planters trowel,
like a piece of table-ware,
her ashes in an earthen jar.
Just beyond, a maple tree,
a stone at its base.

The minister, silken stole around his shoulders,
giving the moment a cloak of solemnity,
began his eulogy with words pouring out
like cans of fruit on a pantry shelf,
in their proper order.

After taking up the ashes,
he began to pour at the hole,
turning to the husband,
offering him the earthen jar,
for him to show his condolences,
 inviting me to do the same.

Hoping Ann wouldn't mind my taking liberties,
I accepted his request
began to pour,
then saw the stone by the tree.

Suddenly it is I falling down the hole,
caught in a whirlpool, falling faster and faster,
seeing the image of a little girl,
among those who were teasing me,
on their way from school.

She stepped out from behind a maple tree
catching my stone at her brow.
In my horror at my deed,
I could only say she stepped out from the tree.
No one listening to the little boy's cry:
please forgive me.

Then, it was over. I was back,
saying good-by to a friend, her plaque
now on the memorial garden wall.

# A Meditation

On the river's bridge one night
I stopped to meditate,
reflecting on other bridges I had crossed,
while I watched the swollen currents below.

Swirling, splashing, heedless,
my path in retrospect—
not stopping.

Could I, at what seemed an inclement course,
have stayed a bit longer,
caught the trace of trouble in your eyes?

Like the river, I didn't slow,
but learned, painfully so,
too late you closed your life.

# Faith

A friend said *Come follow me.*
*See what I've found in the woods.*
We came upon a clapboard-sided church.
It looked to be a hundred years old, or more.
Its steeple about to topple.

To the entrance we climbed the broken steps,
squeezing through a pair of doors
partly off their hinges.

Inside, except for dust and fallen plaster,
rows of pews still in place. It seemed
the people may have just gone home
for supper after church.

No hymn manuals to tell us what they sang,
except for a broken-down pump organ.
At the front, where a minister of stature
may have stood, was a stepstool
at the now silenced rostrum.

There was no sign of their denomination,
bare walls, the lack of statuary
and empty coat hangers along the sides,
gave hint of their austerity.

Pieces of twisted crepe paper
still clung to nails in the rafters, indicating
there may have been a celebration
or final meeting at their church's demise.

Or was this story but a metaphor?

Peter Olevnik

## A Holy Place

I like to take a morning walk
to a special place
just after sunrise, when the stillness
fills my mind and eyes.

As I reach the top of the hill,
the street continues down
to meet the trees beyond
where they in turn begin to ascend
the mountain side.

Where they cease, the mountain
continues on its climb, arriving
at a plateau mantled in morning mist,
pillow like, where the mountain breaks
on its way to crest.

As the morning sun
climbs the mountain's other side,
the sky stretches out in marbled hues,
with sunlit clouds etched in flame,
I taste the sweetness
of the morning mountain air,
and know I'm in a holy place.

## The Carrion

My dear carrion caught
in lights of an indifferent crowd
I troubled to avoid—
too late in your search for safety
to get to the other side.
By your fate, another dined.

My dear carrion
you might have hesitated,
heading up the highway.
Unvarying in direction,
you took the tragic road.

There will be no arrest,
no all-points bulletin,
nor funeral: in a day or two
there will be no evidence
that all you wanted
was to try another side.

No one will mourn your passing,
seek your designation
as an endangered species,
or record you as a frail
body pulled from
a bombed or shaken building.
I will mourn your loss as mine.

# Sunset

An early, warm October evening
with the sky awash in phthalo hues,
brushed in glazes of pink and rose,
with daylight, sponged the air.

Distant trees, like banners in bars of green,
stair-stepped in our perception,
striding up the mountain side, each row
more gently bathed in ascending blues.

The sun, at day's declining hour,
set ablaze in a golden fringe
like lace along the mountain top,
at sunset slipping further down the other side.

Wafting above the setting sun
a braid of cloud in light entwined
its skirt alit in yellow, orange and red,
a Turner sky, in awe I end the day.

# BOOK IV
# Addendum

Peter Olevnik

# A Fable Revisited

The way the story goes, Jack and Jill were headed up a hill for a pail of water. Jack fell down and silly Jill right behind him, getting caught up in the moment, not seeing a rock, also took a tumble.

Perhaps we have it all wrong and she was actually racing Jack to get there first. Not like Jack's companion. In a dream I had, my friend showed compassion when I fell. My mother would have scolded me for being in a rush to climb the hill. The pals I hang with wouldn't buy the story in the first place. Hadn't Jack heard of a faucet?

## Rumpelstiltskin Revisited

I am a heap of straw
piled high against a barren wall.
Somehow, it's with your touch
I am, from your spinning wheel,
charged to turn straw to golden verse.

Because of your mentor's boast,
you are confined to your writing desk
and I to form some lines of straw.
A hapless task!

If only I could offer you a poem,
a heap lying at your feet,
and be that muse
propel your fingers to spin a golden ode,
I would.

Buried Pennies

# About the Author

Peter Olevnik grew up in Fort Wayne, a former manufacturing center at the confluence of three rivers in northeastern Indiana. He spent most of his working years as a university librarian in Illinois and New York, receiving his PhD at the State University of NY at Buffalo.

*Buried Pennies* is Peter's second book of poetry, following his anthology of poems and stories titled *Look Homeward Asheville* (Grateful Steps, 2009), which was nominated for the Thomas Wolfe Memorial Literary Award. Peter's love of writing is reflected in his role as facilitator, and participant, in the annual "Poetry Sunday" celebration of poems presented by members of the Unitarian-Universalist Congregation of Asheville, and in his role in establishing the continuing "Poetry Lovers" participant gathering at the Osher Lifelong Learning Institute, University of North Carolina Asheville.

Peter is also an accomplished painter and portraitist, having shown his works in galleries and exhibitions in several states including Illinois, Indiana, New York, and North Carolina.

Since retirement, Peter and his wife, Judy, have made their home in Asheville, North Carolina.

## For poetry lovers, from Pisgah Press

Letting Go: Collected Poems 1983-2003 — 978-0985387501
$14.95 — Donna Lisle Burton

Way Past Time for Reflecting — 978-1942016281
$17.95 — Donna Lisle Burton

Invasive Procedures: Earthquakes, Calamities, & poems from the midst of life — 978-1942016229
$17.95 — Nan Socolow

## Memoir

I Like It Here! Adventures in the Wild & Wonderful World of Theatre — 978-0985387563
$30.00 — C. Robert Jones

Unbelievable: Faith, Reason, & the Search for Truth — 978-0615517377
$16.00 — Joseph R. Haun

A Green One for Woody — 978-0985387549
$15.95 — Patrick O'Sullivan

## Fiction

Trang Sen: A Novel of Vietnam — Sarah-Ann Smith
$19.50

THE RICK RYDER MYSTERY SERIES — RF Wilson
Deadly Dancing — 978-1942016151
$15.95
Killer Weed — 978-1942016267
$14.95

## Non-fiction

Red-state, White-guy Blues — 978-1942016045
$15.95 — Jeff Douglas Messer

Reed's Homophones: a comprehensive book of sound-alike words — 978-0985387518
$10.00 — A.D. Reed

Swords in Their Hands: George Washington and the Newburgh Conspiracy — 978-0985387587
$24.95 — Dave Richards

## To order:

Pisgah Press, LLC
PO Box 1427, Candler, NC 28715
www.pisgahpress.com

www.ingramcontent.com/pod-product-compliance
Lightning Source LLC
LaVergne TN
LVHW051849080426
835512LV00018B/3160